Uncle Shelby's ABZ Book

a primer for tender young minds

by Shel Silverstein

A FIRESIDE BOOK

PUBLISHED BY SIMON & SCHUSTER, INC.

NEW YORK

A portion of this book originally appeared in *Playboy* Magazine in a slightly different form, and is used by arrangement with the HMH Publishing Company.

First Fireside Edition, 1961

Published by Simon & Schuster, Inc.

Rockefeller Center
1230 Avenue of the Americas
New York, New York 10020

FIRESIDE and colophon are registered trademarks
of Simon & Schuster, Inc.

Manufactured in the United States of America

30 29 28 27 26 25 24

Library of Congress Cataloging in Publication Data

Silverstein, Shel.
  Uncle Shelby's ABZ book.

  "A portion of this book originally appeared in
Playboy magazine in a slightly different form"—T.p.
verso.
  "A Fireside book."
  1. American wit and humor. I. Title. II. Title:
ABZ book.
PN6162.S525 1985   818'.5402   85-14242
ISBN 0-671-21148-X Pbk.

THIS BOOK IS AFFECTIONATELY DEDICATED
TO UNCLE SHELBY'S OLD COMRADE,

JEAN SHEPHERD.

Poem

↓

O CHILD LEARN YOUR ABZ'S
AND MEMORIZE THEM WELL
AND YOU SHALL LEARN TO TALK AND THINK
AND READ AND WRITE AND SPEL.

A Book For You

MANY OF MY LITTLE FRIENDS HAVE ASKED OLD UNCLE SHELBY WHY HE HAS WRITTEN THIS BOOK AND WHY HE LOVES CHILDREN SO DEARLY, AND TO THESE I MUST ANSWER THAT ALTHOUGH UNCLE SHELBY HAS NEVER BEEN BLESSED WITH CHILDREN OF HIS OWN, THE LITTLE ONES HAVE ALWAYS HAD A VERY SPECIAL PLACE IN HIS TIRED OLD HEART.

YES, I HAVE HEARD THEM CRYING LATE AT NIGHT, AND I HAVE THOUGHT ABOUT THEM—

I HAVE HEARD THEM PLAYING AND LAUGH-ING OUTSIDE MY WINDOW WHILE I WAS TRYING TO SLEEP AND I HAVE THOUGHT ABOUT THEM—

I HAVE SEEN THE PICTURES THEY HAVE DRAWN ON MY CAR AND I HAVE THOUGHT AND THOUGHT AND THOUGHT ABOUT THEM.

AND SO THIS BOOK—

TO HELP ALL MY LITTLE FRIENDS GET ALL THE THINGS IN LIFE THAT THEY SO RICHLY DESERVE.

YOUR OWN, *Uncle Shelby*

A IS FOR APPLE

SEE THE NICE
GREEN APPLE.
M-M-M-M-GOOD.

HOW MANY NICE GREEN
APPLES CAN YOU EAT ?
MAKE A CIRCLE AROUND THE NUMBER
OF NICE GREEN LITTLE APPLES
YOU ATE TODAY.
1 2 3 4 7 12 26 38 57 83 91 116

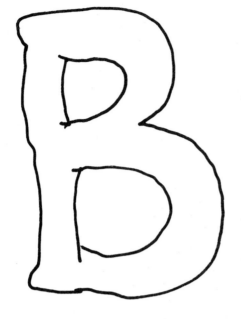 **IS FOR BABY**

SEE THE BABY
THE BABY IS FAT
THE BABY IS PINK
THE BABY CAN CRY
THE BABY CAN LAUGH
SEE THE BABY PLAY
PLAY, BABY, PLAY.
PRETTY, PRETTY, BABY.

MOMMY LOVES THE BABY

MORE THAN SHE LOVES YOU.

BABY ←

 IS FOR ZOO

LET'S GO TO THE ZOO
SEE ALL THE ANIMALS!
THE ANIMALS ARE LOCKED
INSIDE THE CAGES.
POOR ANIMALS!
WHO WILL LET THEM OUT???

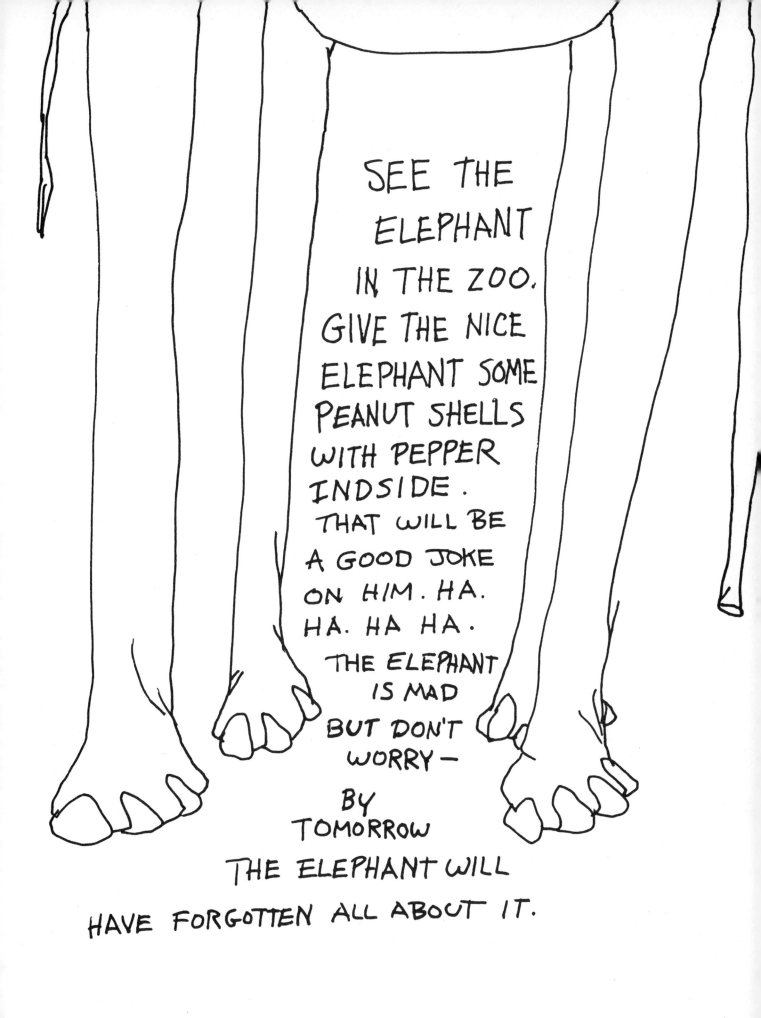

SEE THE
ELEPHANT
IN THE ZOO.
GIVE THE NICE
ELEPHANT SOME
PEANUT SHELLS
WITH PEPPER
INDSIDE.
THAT WILL BE
A GOOD JOKE
ON HIM. HA.
HA. HA HA.
THE ELEPHANT
IS MAD
BUT DON'T
WORRY —
BY
TOMORROW
THE ELEPHANT WILL
HAVE FORGOTTEN ALL ABOUT IT.

POOR HIPPOPOTOMUS. THE HIPPOPOTUMOS
HAS A BONE STUCK IN HIS THROAT AND
CAN'T GET IT OUT. POOR HIPOPOTHOMUS
THE HIPOPOTTOMOS HAS NO FINGERS
LIKE YOU DO. POOR HIPOTOPOMUS.
SAY, MAYBE HE IS NOT A REAL HIPTOPOMOS
AFTER ALL. MAYBE
HE IS REALLY A
ROYAL PRINCE
THAT HAS BEEN
TURNED INTO
A HIPOPOTOMOS
BY A WICKED
WITCH AND WHEN
SOME PERSON TAKES THE
BONE OUT OF HIS THROAT
THE SPELL WILL BE BROKEN
AND HE WILL TURN BACK
INTO A PRINCE AGAIN AND GIVE
WHOEVER
DID IT
A MILLION
DOLLARS IN
GOLD AND A HORSE AND A CASTLE.

SEE THE HIPPOPOTIMUS

IN
THE
ZOO

WHEW!

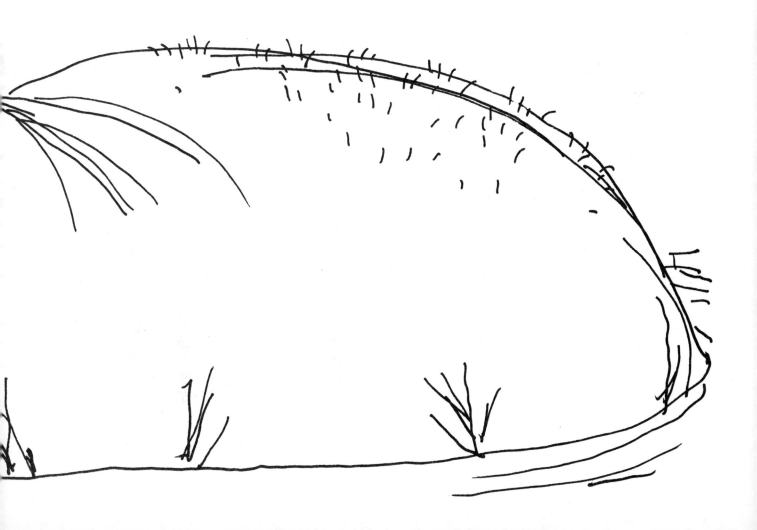

SEE THE NICE TIGER
IN THE ZOO
THE TIGER IS PEEKING
OUT OF THE GRASS
AT YOU AND —
SAY—
THERE IS NO GRASS IN THE
ZOO

WHERE ARE THE IRON CAGES?
THERE ARE NO CAGES.

HEY, THIS IS NO ZOO
THIS IS THE JUNGLE..
AND ALL THOSE WILD ANIMALS ARE
LOOSE
AND YOU'D BETTER RUN
FAST...!

OK, Kids LET'S ALL..

SING ALONG WITH UNCLE SHELBY

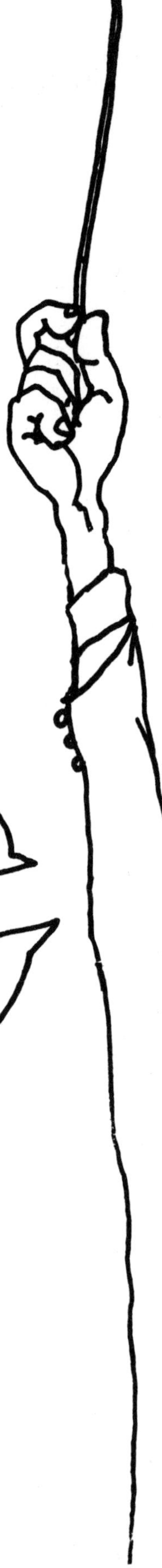

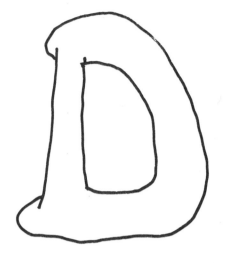

D IS FOR DADDY

SEE DADDY.

SEE DADDY *SLEEPING ON THE COUCH?*

SEE DADDY'S HAIR

DADDY NEEDS A HAIRCUT

POOR DADDY. DADDY HAS NO MONEY FOR
A HAIRCUT.

DADDY SPENDS ALL HIS MONEY TO BUY
YOU TOYS AND OATMEAL.

POOR DADDY. DADDY CAN NOT HAVE A
HAIRCUT.

POOR POOR DADDY

SEE THE SCISSORS...

POOR POOR POOR POOR
DADDY.

 IS FOR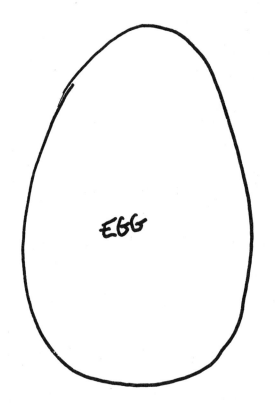

EGG

SEE THE EGG.
THE EGG IS
FULL OF SLIMEY
GOOEY WHITE
STUFF AND ICKY
YELLOW STUFF.
DO YOU LIKE
TO EAT EGGS?

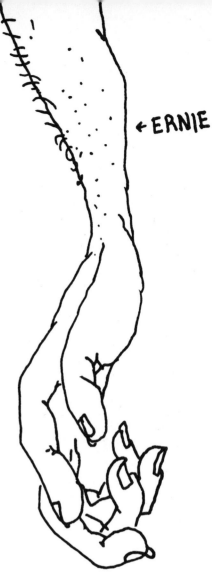

← ERNIE

IS ALSO FOR ERNIE.
ERNIE IS THE GENIE WHO
LIVES IN THE CEILING.
ERNIE LOVES EGGS.
TAKE A NICE FRESH EGG AND THROW
IT AS HIGH AS YOU CAN AND YELL
" CATCH, ERNIE "
" CATCH THE EGG ! "

AND ERNIE WILL REACH DOWN AND
CATCH THE EGG.

SEE THE FINGERS.

CAN YOU COUNT YOUR FINGERS?

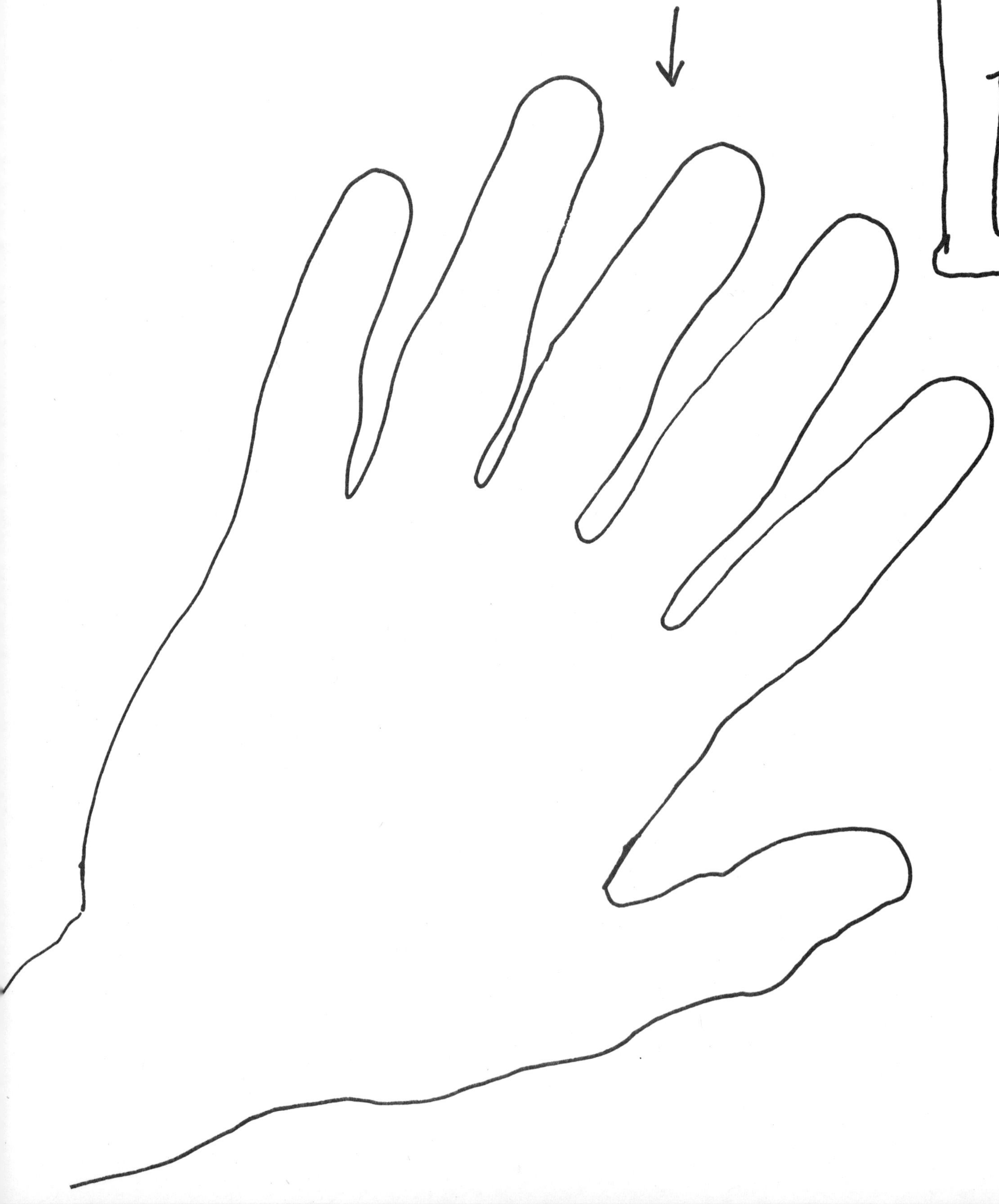

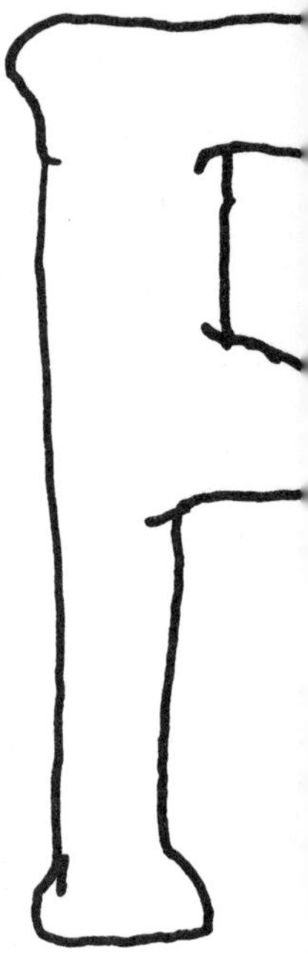

IS FOR FINGER

FINGERS ARE FUN
YOU CAN STICK YOUR FINGER INTO YOUR
NOSE.

DOESN'T THAT FEEL NICE?
YOU CAN STICK YOUR FINGER INTO THE BABY'S EAR.
THE BABY IS CRYING.
MAYBE HE WANTS HIS BOTTLE.
YOU CAN STICK YOUR FINGER INTO THE FIRE—
OOH — THE FIRE IS HOT
QUICK— STICK YOUR FINGER INTO THE MAYONNAISE!
—THERE, ISN'T THAT NICE AND COOL?
PRINT C-O-O-L ON THE MIRROR
IN MAYONNAISE.
AREN'T FINGERS FUN?
TOMORROW WE WILL FIND SOME NEW
THINGS TO DO WITH FINGERS.

AND NOW IT'S TIME FOR HANDICRAFT CLASS AND THIS MORNING UNCLE SHELBY IS GOING TO TEACH YOU HOW TO MAKE YOUR OWN VOODOO DOLLY PIN CUSHION

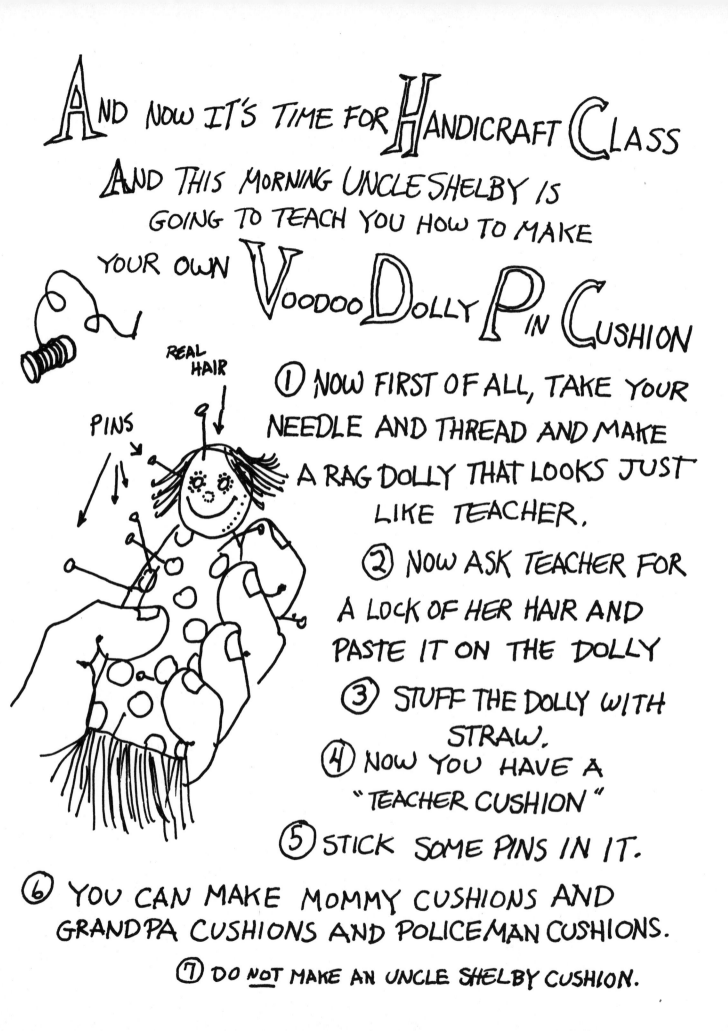

REAL HAIR

PINS

① NOW FIRST OF ALL, TAKE YOUR NEEDLE AND THREAD AND MAKE A RAG DOLLY THAT LOOKS JUST LIKE TEACHER.

② NOW ASK TEACHER FOR A LOCK OF HER HAIR AND PASTE IT ON THE DOLLY

③ STUFF THE DOLLY WITH STRAW.

④ NOW YOU HAVE A "TEACHER CUSHION"

⑤ STICK SOME PINS IN IT.

⑥ YOU CAN MAKE MOMMY CUSHIONS AND GRANDPA CUSHIONS AND POLICEMAN CUSHIONS.

⑦ DO NOT MAKE AN UNCLE SHELBY CUSHION.

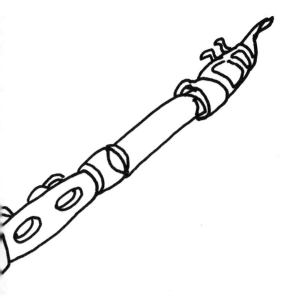

SEE THE PRETTY GIGOLO.
THE GIGOLO MAKES BEAUTIFUL MUSIC.
THE NEXT TIME YOUR MOMMY GOES SHOPPING,
ASK HER TO BUY YOU A GIGOLO.
SHE WILL TELL ALL THE NEIGHBORS HOW
CUTE YOU ARE
AND SHE WILL WRITE IT IN TO THE
READER'S DIGEST
AND THEY WILL PRINT IT AND SEND
YOU MONEY.

H IS FOR HOLE

SEE THE HOLE

THE HOLE IS DEEP

YOU CAN BURY THINGS IN THE HOLE.

SEE THE TOASTER.

YOU CAN BURY THE TOASTER IN THE HOLE.

SEE THE CAR KEYS.

DEEP HOLE →

YOU CAN BURY THE CAR KEYS
    IN THE HOLE.

SEE GRANDMA'S TEETH
SEE DADDY'S SHOE
SEE MOMMY'S DIAMOND RING

OH-OH-LITTLE SISTER* SEES
YOU BURYING THINGS IN THE
    HOLE

MAYBE SHE WILL SWITCH ON
YOU AND YOU WILL GET A
    LICKING.

WHAT
    ELSE
    CAN YOU
        BURY IN THE
            HOLE....?

I IS FOR INK

INK IS BLACK AND WET.
INK IS FUN.

WHAT CAN YOU DO
WITH INK?

WHAT RHYMES WITH INK?

"DR____"

K

IS FOR KIDNAPPER

SEE THE NICE KIDNAPPER

THE KIDNAPPER HAS A LOLLIPOP.

THE KIDNAPPER HAS A KEEN CAR.

THE CAR CAN GO FAST.

TELL THE NICE KIDNAPPER THAT YOUR DADDY HAS LOTS OF MONEY. THEN MAYBE HE WILL LET YOU RIDE IN HIS CAR.

IT'S QUESTION TIME

DO YOU WANT TO BE SMART?

ASK SOME QUESTIONS

ASK DADDY WHY THE SKY
IS BLUE.

ASK TEACHER WHERE DO BABIES
COME FROM.

ASK MOMMY WHY DADDY COMES
HOME LATE FROM WORK.

ASK ASK ASK ASK ASK ASK ASK
ASK ASK ASK ASK ASK ASK
ASK ASK ASK ASK ASK ASK
ASK ASK ASK ASK AS
ASK ASK ASK ASK

Now It's Drawing Time

YES KIDS IT'S TIME TO DRAW SO TAKE OUT YOUR
PENCILS AND CRAYONS AND CHALK AND DRAW
SOMETHING NICE ON THE WHOLE PAGE. IT'S JUST FOR YOU
AND NEVER MIND THE WITCH — SHE SAID THAT THIS IS HER PAGE
AND IF ANYBODY DREW ON IT SHE'D TURN THEM INTO A RAT.
BUT I DON'T BELIEVE IN WITCHES. DO YOU?

NO OF COURSE NOT... NOW DRAW...... DRAW....?..

J IS FOR JOKE
DO YOU KNOW A
FUNNY JOKE?
HERE IS WHAT TO SAY;

"ONCE UPON A TIME THERE WAS A
TRAVELING SALESMAN WHO STOPPED AT
A FARMERS HOUSE ....

(SEE—DADDY LOOKS SURPRISED
DADDY DIDN'T KNOW YOU KNEW A JOKE)

"AND THE FARMER SAID YOU'll HAVE
TO SLEEP WITH MY DAUGHTER........

(SEE.. DADDY LOOKS FUNNY)
DADDY IS SWEATING

"AND THE SALESMAN SAID I
DON'T WANT TO SLEEP ANYWHERE
I WANT TO KNOW WHICH WAY IT IS
TO KENOSHA AND THE FARMER TOLD
HIM AND HE WENT AWAY. THE END.

(SEE—DADDY IS SMILING—
THAT WAS A VERY FUNNY JOKE!

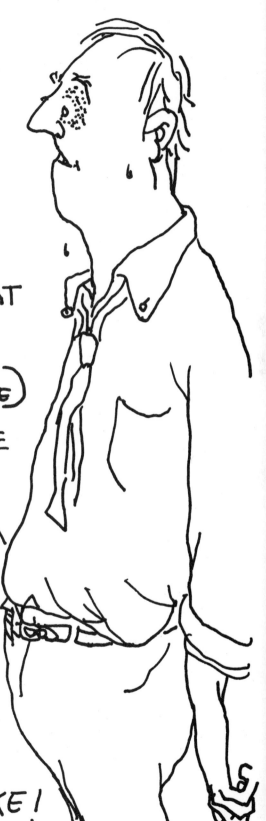

MERRY XMAS KIDS

AND HERE IS UNCLE SHELBY'S
CHRISTMAS PRESENT TO YOU
A SHINEY NEW QUARTER
AND I PASTED IT ON HERE MYSELF

SO HAVE FUN AND BUY ANYTHING YOU WANT
Yoous Truly
Uncle Shelby

P.S.- I HOPE YOUR MOMMY DOESN'T TAKE THE QUARTER OFF AND KEEP IT!

IS FOR MONEY

MOMMY AND DADDY ALWAYS FIGHT
ABOUT MONEY.

MONEY IS THE ROOT OF ALL EVIL.
SEE THE MONEY.   THE MONEY IS GREEN.
THE MONEY IS IN MOMMY'S PURSE.
TAKE THE BAD BAD MONEY OUT OF THE PURSE
AND SEND IT TO P.O. BOX 42, St. LOUIS, MISSOURI.

THEN MOMMY AND DADDY WILL BE HAPPY.

NO, THIS IS <u>NOT</u> A FRYING PAN!
IT IS <u>NOT</u> A LOOKING GLASS!
IT IS <u>NOT</u> A PING-PONG
PADDLE!

STOP TRYING TO BE
A SMART ALEC!

IS FOR LOLLIPOP!

LOLLIPOPS ARE GOOD
TO EAT JUST BEFORE
SUPPER!

L IS ALSO FOR

DO YOU WANT A NICE RED LOLLIPOP?
GO POUR ALL THE LYE INTO THE TOILET.
NOW TELL MOMMY YOU HAVE EATEN *THE LYE*
(THAT IS A FIB OR A LITTLE WHITE LYE)

MOMMY WILL TAKE YOU TO THE DOCTOR
IN A TAXI CAB.
AFTER THE DOCTOR PUMPS OUT
YOUR STOMACH,
HE WILL GIVE YOU A NICE RED LOLLIPOP.

WELL, NOW...

ALL MY LITTLE FRIENDS HAVE BEEN
ASKING ME THE SAME QUESTION,
"UNCLE SHELBY, WHERE DO BABIES
                        COME FROM?

MOMMY AND DADDY
WON'T TELL US!"

WELL, NEVER FEAR, MY SWEET ONES,

YOUR GOOD OLD UNCLE SHELBY

WILL
        TELL
                YOU.....

DO YOU SEE THIS ANIMAL?
DO YOU KNOW WHAT IT IS?
IT IS A <u>STORK</u>.

THE STORK MIGHT
BE A BIRDIE....
THE STORK MIGHT
BE A FISHY....
THE STORK HAS WINGS AND
FEET AND A BEAK LIKE A
BIRDIE.....
BUT THE STORK BRINGS LITTLE
BABIES FROM HEAVEN AND
DROPS THEM DOWN THE
CHIMNEY.
DOESN'T THAT SOUND A LITTLE
FISHY TO YOU.....?

IS

FOR

NOSE

DID YOU EVER HEAR OF
PINOCCHIO?
WELL, PINOCCHIO WAS A
PUPPET

WHO LIKED TO TELL LIES
AND EVERY TIME HE TOLD A LIE
HIS NOSE WOULD GROW LONGER AND LONGER
DO YOU THINK THAT WOULD
HAPPEN TO YOU?
TELL A LITTLE LIE AND SEE WHAT HAPPENS
NOTHING HAPPENED?
DID YOUR NOSE GET LONG?
NO?
ISN'T IT FUN NOT BEING A PUPPET?.!

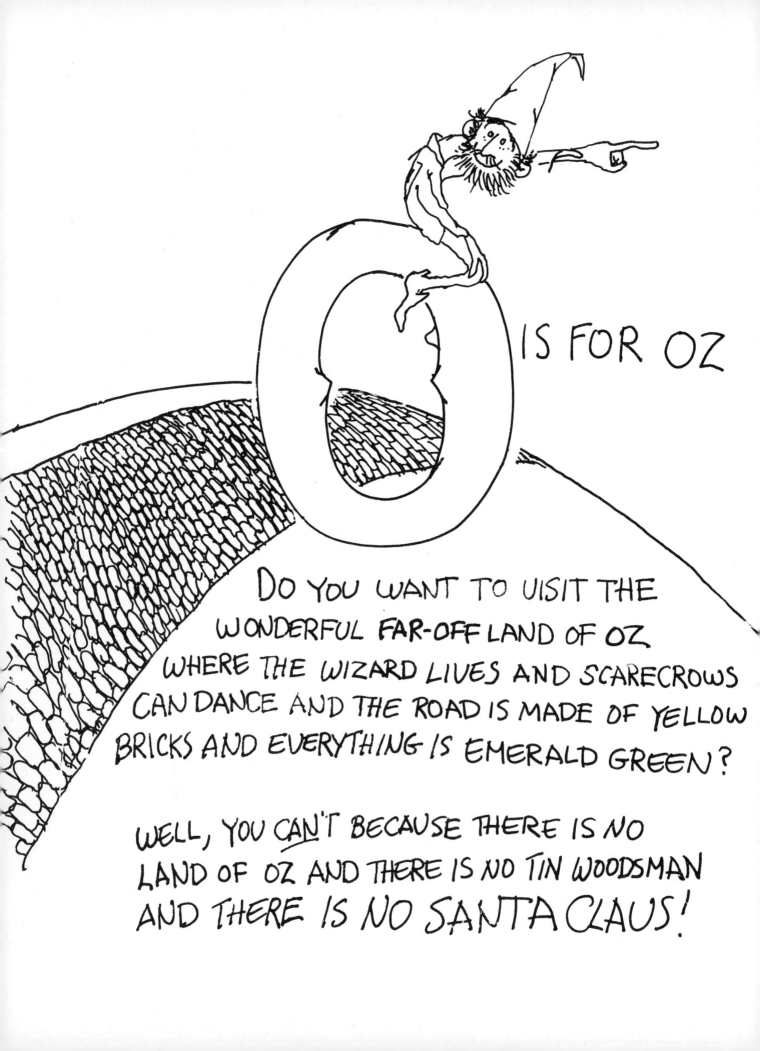

IS FOR OZ

DO YOU WANT TO VISIT THE
WONDERFUL FAR-OFF LAND OF OZ
WHERE THE WIZARD LIVES AND SCARECROWS
CAN DANCE AND THE ROAD IS MADE OF YELLOW
BRICKS AND EVERYTHING IS EMERALD GREEN?

WELL, YOU CAN'T BECAUSE THERE IS NO
LAND OF OZ AND THERE IS NO TIN WOODSMAN
AND THERE IS NO SANTA CLAUS!

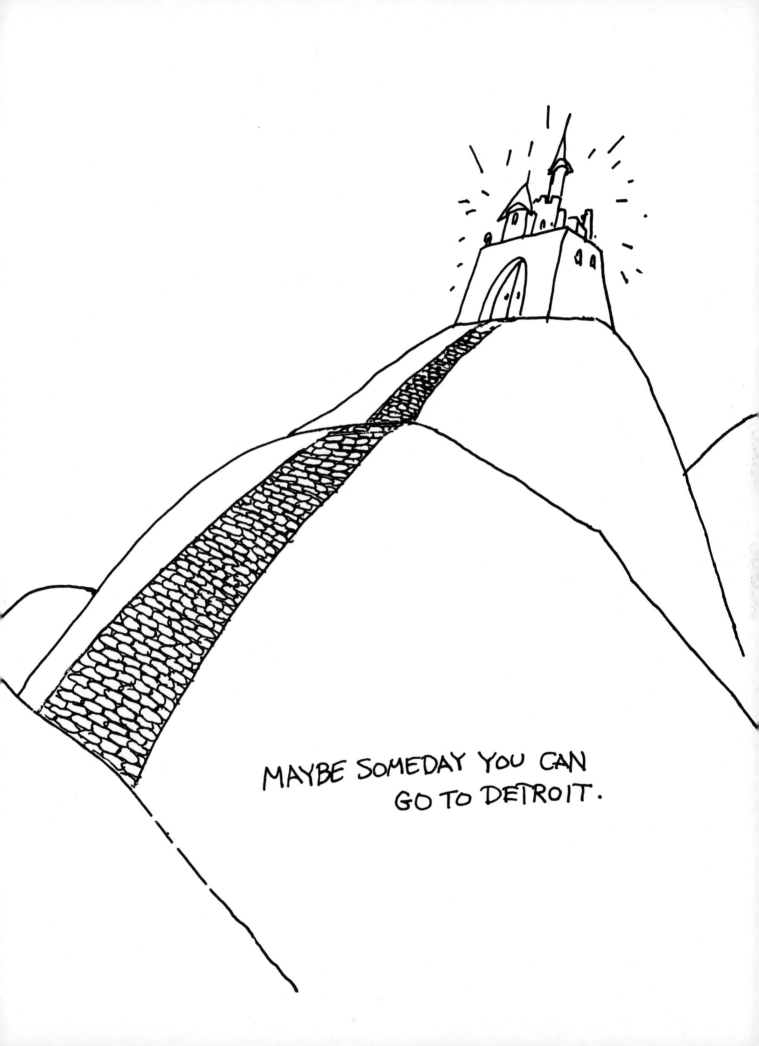

MAYBE SOMEDAY YOU CAN
GO TO DETROIT.

NOW IT'S TIME TO BRUSH OUR TEETH
HOW DO WE BRUSH?
UP AND DOWN? NO! ALWAYS ACROSS!
ACROSS IS MORE FUN!
IF YOU DO NOT BRUSH YOUR TEETH
THEY WILL GET DULL AND YELLOW.
IF YOU BRUSH THEM THEY WILL
BE NICE AND WHITE AND BRIGHT.

MAYBE A WILD BLACK PANTHER WILL
CRAWL IN YOUR WINDOW SOME DARK
NIGHT AND LOOK AROUND FOR SOMEONE
TO EAT BUT HE WON'T SEE YOU BECAUSE
IT'S TOO DARK AND THEN HE WILL SEE
YOUR BRIGHT WHITE TEETH SHINING IN
THE
DARK AND..

IT'S STORY HOUR

NOW IT'S TIME TO CLIMB UP INTO GRANDMA'S BIG SOFT LAP AND HAVE HER TELL YOU A WONDERFUL STORY.

DON'T YOU LOVE GRANDMA? GRANDMA TELLS WONDERFUL STORIES.

DO YOU KNOW THE STORY OF LITTLE RED RIDING HOOD?

(DID YOU EVER NOTICE WHAT BIG TEETH GRANDMA HAS?)

P IS FOR PONY

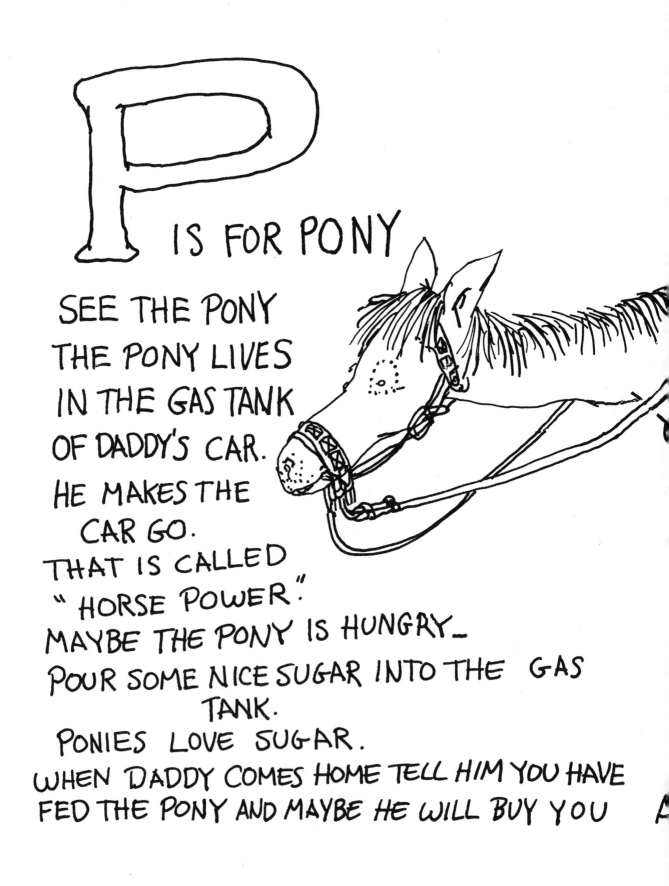

SEE THE PONY
THE PONY LIVES
IN THE GAS TANK
OF DADDY'S CAR.

HE MAKES THE
CAR GO.
THAT IS CALLED
" HORSE POWER."
MAYBE THE PONY IS HUNGRY—
POUR SOME NICE SUGAR INTO THE GAS
TANK.
PONIES LOVE SUGAR.
WHEN DADDY COMES HOME TELL HIM YOU HAVE
FED THE PONY AND MAYBE HE WILL BUY YOU

COWBOY SUIT.

KNOW YOUR ANIMALS
#1 DOGGY

SEE THE NICE DOGGY
THE DOGGY'S NAME IS SPOT
THE DOGGY LOVES YOU
CALL THE DOGGY

"HERE, DOGGY, HERE, SPOT,
HERE, BOY."
MAKE "NICE DOGGY"
DOGGIES LIKE TO BE
SCRATCHED BEHIND
THEIR EARS.

 IS FOR

QUARANTINE

ISN'T THIS A BIG WORD?

DO YOU KNOW WHAT THIS WORD MEANS?

IT MEANS—

COME IN KIDS—
FREE ICE CREAM

R IS FOR RED

THE FIRE IS RED
THE FIRE ENGINE IS RED
THE FIREMAN'S HAT
IS RED

DOES THE FIREMAN IN
THE RED HAT COME TO
YOUR HOUSE IN HIS RED
FIRE ENGINE?
NO?
TOO BAD
THE FIREMAN ONLY
GOES TO PLACES
WHERE THERE IS
A FIRE.

And Now It's....

GAME TIME

YESSIREE
SHOOTERS IT'S
AND TODAY
IS HOP-SCO
WE'RE GOING
SCOTCH SO
DOWN IN THE
THE FLOOR A
HIGH YOU CA

STRAIGHT
GAME TIME
THE GAME
TCH AND
TO USE REAL
PUT THE SCOTCH
MIDDLE OF
ND SEE HOW
N HOP OVER

IT. IF YOU WANT TO HOP HIGHER JUST
TASTE A LITTLE OF THE SCOTCH -M·M·M-
GOOD! ISN'T IT FUN TO PLAY GAMES?

NEXT WEEK WE WILL LEARN TO PLAY DOCTOR.

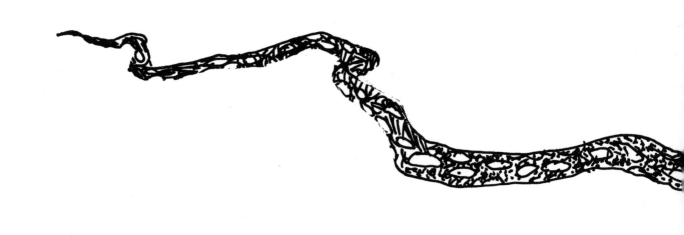

Now it's NAP TIME

DO YOU WANT TO TAKE
A NICE NAP?
IT IS DARK
YOU CAN LISTEN IN THE DARK
WHAT DO YOU HEAR?
DO YOU HEAR THE WEREWOLF?
DO YOU HEAR THE BOOGEY MAN?
DO YOU HEAR THE FANG TOOTH TIGER?

NO NO THERE IS
NOTHING THERE AT ALL,
NOW GO TO SLEEP.

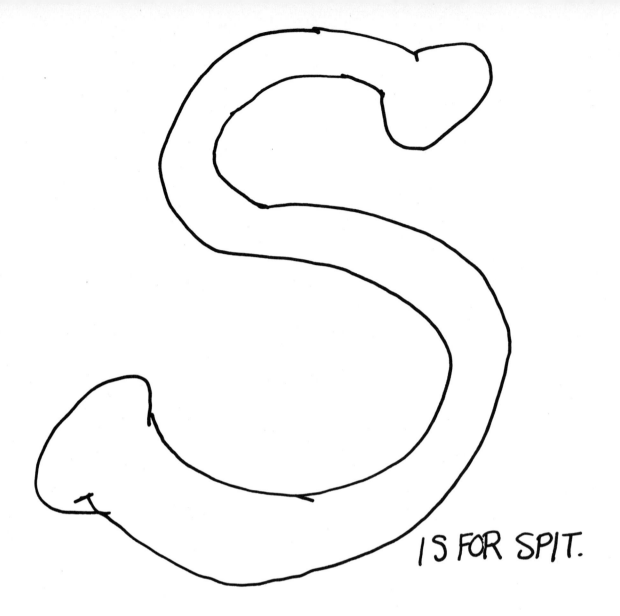

IS FOR SPIT.

THE CHAMPION SPITTER OF THE UNITED STATES OF AMERICA IS RONALD BOGASH AGE II, OF 224 MORTON STREET, CLEVELAND, OHIO.

RONALD SPIT ALL THE WAY FROM THE KITCHEN TO THE LIVING ROOM
☆23 FEET 6¾ INCHES☆

WHO WILL BE THE NEW CHAMPION?

S IS ALSO FOR STANLEY.

STANLEY IS A CRAZY MURDERER WHO LIKES TO MURDER LITTLE BOYS AND GIRLS EARLY <u>S</u>UNDAY MORNING.

ARE YOU AFRAID OF STANLEY?

YOU ARE?

WELL THEN QUICK JUMP OUT OF BED AND GO AND SLEEP WITH MOMMY AND DADDY. THERE-ISN'T THAT BETTER? MOMMY AND DADDY <u>LOVE</u> TO HAVE YOU SLEEP WITH THEM.

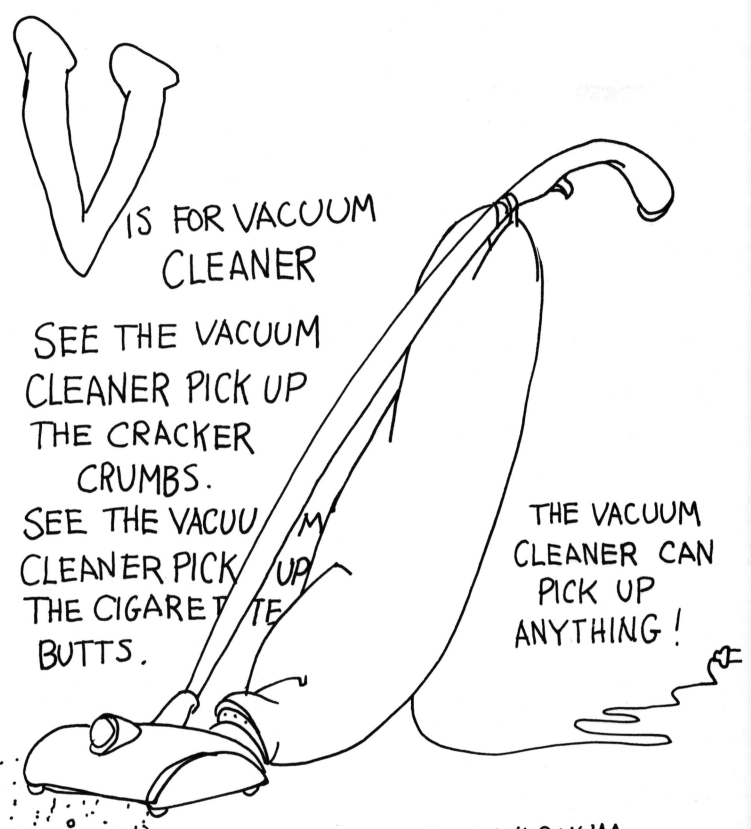

V IS FOR VACUUM CLEANER

SEE THE VACUUM CLEANER PICK UP THE CRACKER CRUMBS.
SEE THE VACUUM CLEANER PICK UP THE CIGARETTE BUTTS.

THE VACUUM CLEANER CAN PICK UP ANYTHING !

DO YOU THINK THE VACUUM CLEANER CAN PICK UP THE CAT?

I DON'T THINK SO...

CUT-OUT TIME

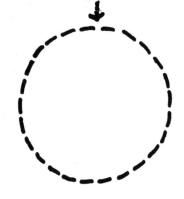

TAKE YOUR SCISSORS AND CUT OUT THIS CIRCLE

↓

CUT ALONG THE DOTTED LINE.

NOW PEEK THROUGH THE HOLE-AND YOU'll BE ABLE TO SEE THE NEXT PAGE!

U IS FOR UNCLE SHELBY

DO YOU LOVE YOUR POOR UNCLE SHELBY?

YES ☐ NO ☐

DO YOU LOVE YOUR ABZ BOOK?

YES ☐ NO ☐

ARE YOU GOING TO BUY UNCLE SHELBY'S NEXT BOOK AND IF YOUR MOMMY WON'T BUY IT FOR YOU ARE YOU GOING TO KICK AND SCREAM AND HOLD YOUR BREATH UNTIL SHE SAYS O.K.?

YES ☐ MAYBE ☐

NOW YOU CAN HAVE SOME CANDY.

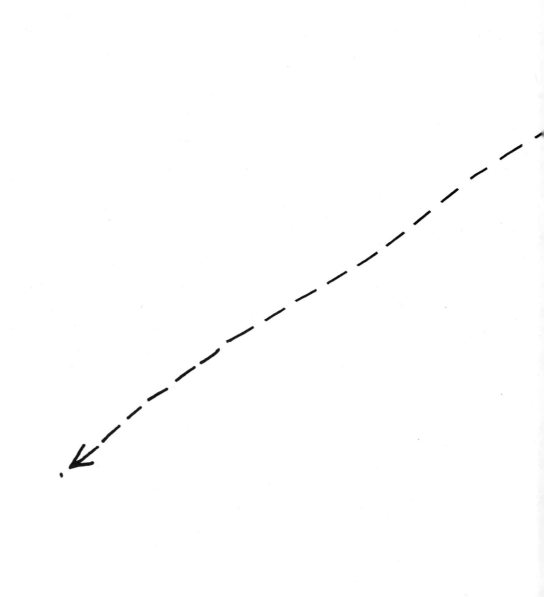

UNCLE SHELBY'S

Pet Parade

SEE THE TERMITE
THE TERMITE IS CRYING "BOO-HOO-HOO"
WHY ARE YOU CRYING, MR. TERMITE?
MR. TERMITE IS CRYING BECAUSE HE IS
LONELY.
MR. TERMITE WANTS TO BE SOMEBODY'S PET
DO YOU HAVE A PET?
TAKE MR. TERMITE HOME IN YOUR POCKET
SHHH— DO NOT MAKE ANY NOISE
PUT HIM IN THE BOTTOM DRAWER OF
YOUR DRESSER.
YOU DO NOT HAVE TO FEED HIM ANYTHING

DO NOT TELL MOMMY OR DADDY
ABOUT YOUR PET TERMITE.

NOW YOU HAVE A
SECRET.

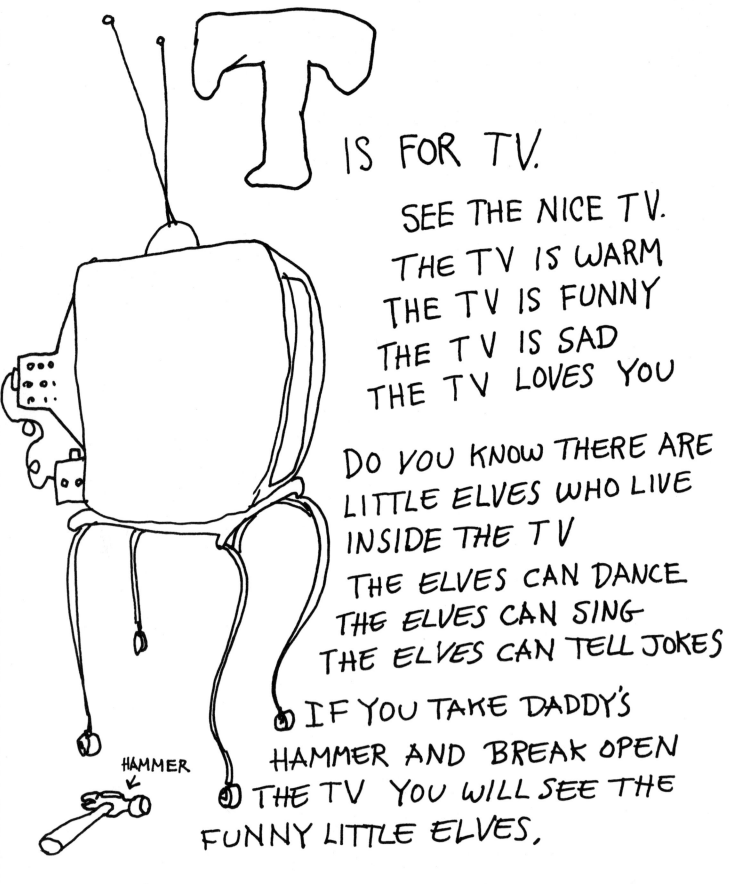

T IS FOR TV.

SEE THE NICE TV.
THE TV IS WARM
THE TV IS FUNNY
THE TV IS SAD
THE TV LOVES YOU

DO YOU KNOW THERE ARE
LITTLE ELVES WHO LIVE
INSIDE THE TV
THE ELVES CAN DANCE
THE ELVES CAN SING
THE ELVES CAN TELL JOKES

IF YOU TAKE DADDY'S
HAMMER AND BREAK OPEN
THE TV YOU WILL SEE THE
FUNNY LITTLE ELVES,

WHAT WILL YOU NAME THEM?

HAMMER

Now it's time for

UNCLE SHELBY'S

Potty Training

SEE THE POTTY.
THE POTTY IS DEEP
THE POTTY HAS WATER
AT THE BOTTOM.

MAYBE SOMEBODY
WILL FALL IN THE
POTTY AND DROWN.

DON'T WORRY,
AS LONG AS YOU
KEEP WETTING YOUR
PANTS, YOU WILL NEVER
DROWN IN THE POTTY.

ACT NOW!

Hey Gang

HURRY!

DO YOU WANT TO

JOIN UNCLE SHELBY'S SECRET CLUB AND GET YOUR FREE CLUB RING AND DE-CODE-O-GRAPH AND CLUB HANDBOOK WITH ALL THE SECRET CODES AND HANDSHAKES AND THE CLUB FLAG AND THE EASY TO ASSEMBLE CLUB CLUB HOUSE AND THE CLUB BADGE WITH THE SECRET COMPARTMENT AND THE CLUB RULES AND THE INVISIBLE INK AND THE UNIFORM AND THE SWORD AND EVERYTHING!!

ALL ENTRIES MUST BE POSTMARKED NO LATER THAN FEB 6, 1934

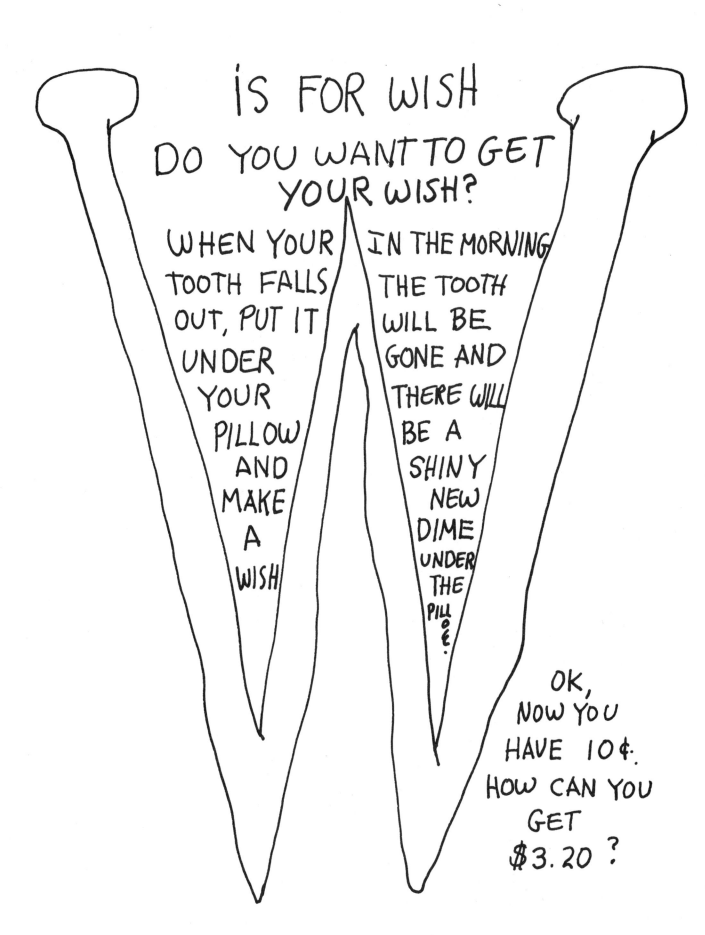

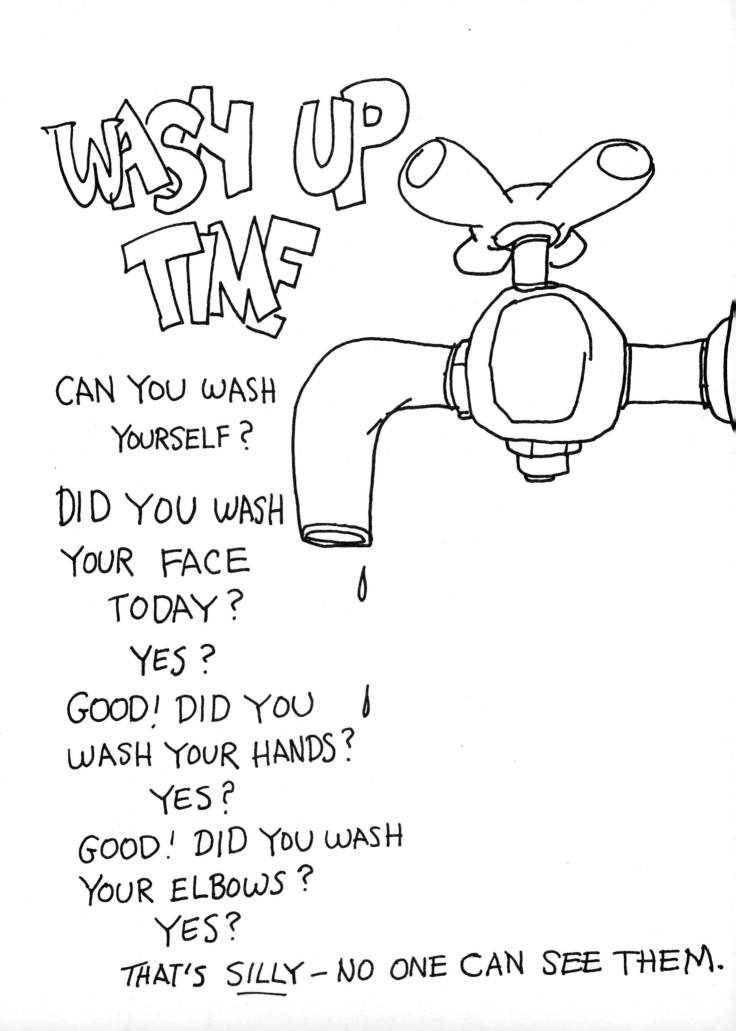

WASH UP TIME

CAN YOU WASH YOURSELF?

DID YOU WASH YOUR FACE TODAY? YES? GOOD! DID YOU WASH YOUR HANDS? YES? GOOD! DID YOU WASH YOUR ELBOWS? YES? THAT'S SILLY — NO ONE CAN SEE THEM.

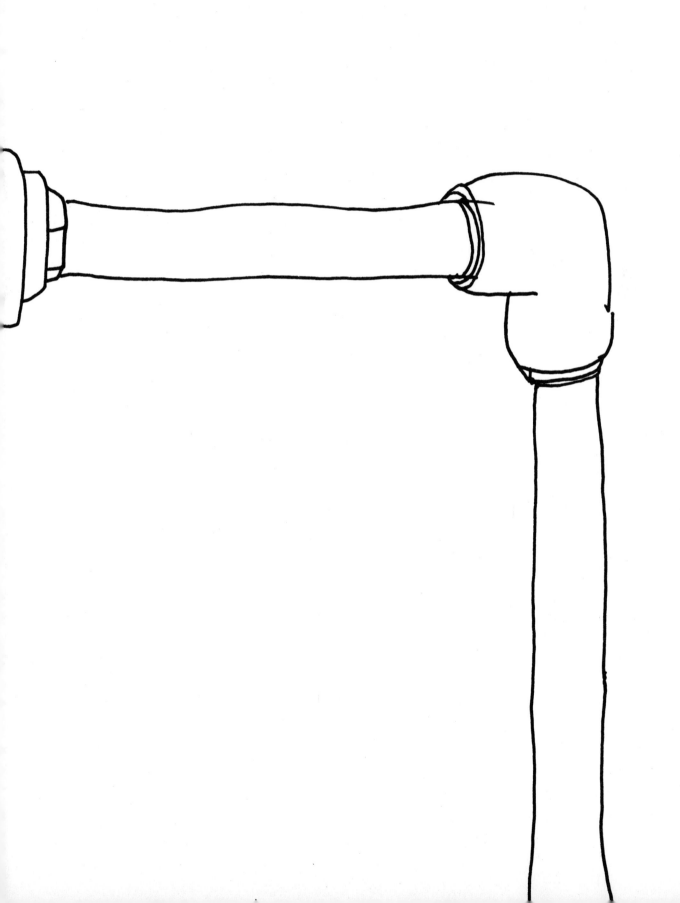

*HI KEEDS -

YEP, IT'S ME, YOUR OLD
PAL THE MAD HATTER
BUT I'M NOT MAD ANY MORE
KEEDS, BECAUSE I'VE QUIT
OLD ALICE AND I'M NOW
WORKING FOR YOUR FRIEND
AND MINE "UNCLE SHELBY"
YES SIR, BOYS AND GIRLS,
UNCLE SHELBY IS A REAL
FRIEND TO LABOR AND
MANAGEMENT BOTH - AND
LOTS OF PEOPLE THINK HE'D
MAKE A SWELL GOVERNOR.
LET'S HEAR IT FOR "UNCLE SHELBY!"

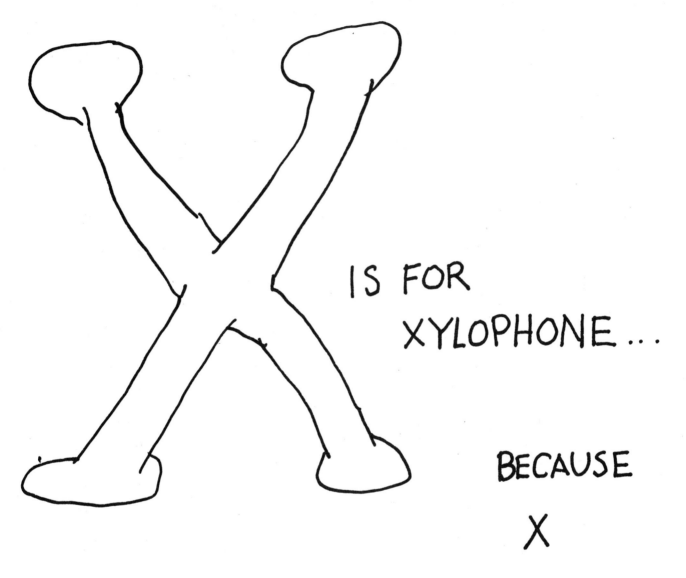

IS FOR

XYLOPHONE...

BECAUSE

X

IS

ALWAYS

FOR

XYLOPHONE!

Did You Learn your ABZ's?

All right, now Uncle Shelby Is going to teach you a

☆ MAGIC WORD ☆

SHHH — THE WORD IS "BOOBOORUBOO"

IF YOU DON'T LIKE TO WASH INSIDE YOUR EARS, JUST SAY THE MAGIC WORD "BOOBOORUBOO" AND YOU WILL NEVER HAVE TO WASH THEM AGAIN BECAUSE THEY WILL STAY CLEAN FOR EVER AND EVER.

ISN'T MAGIC FUN?

Y IS FOR YELL

HOW LOUD CAN
YOU
YELL?

THIS BOOK IS FOR THE KID WHO CAN YELL THE LOUDEST.

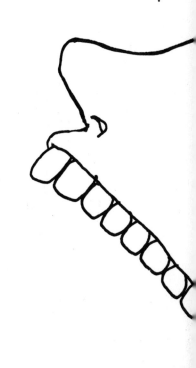

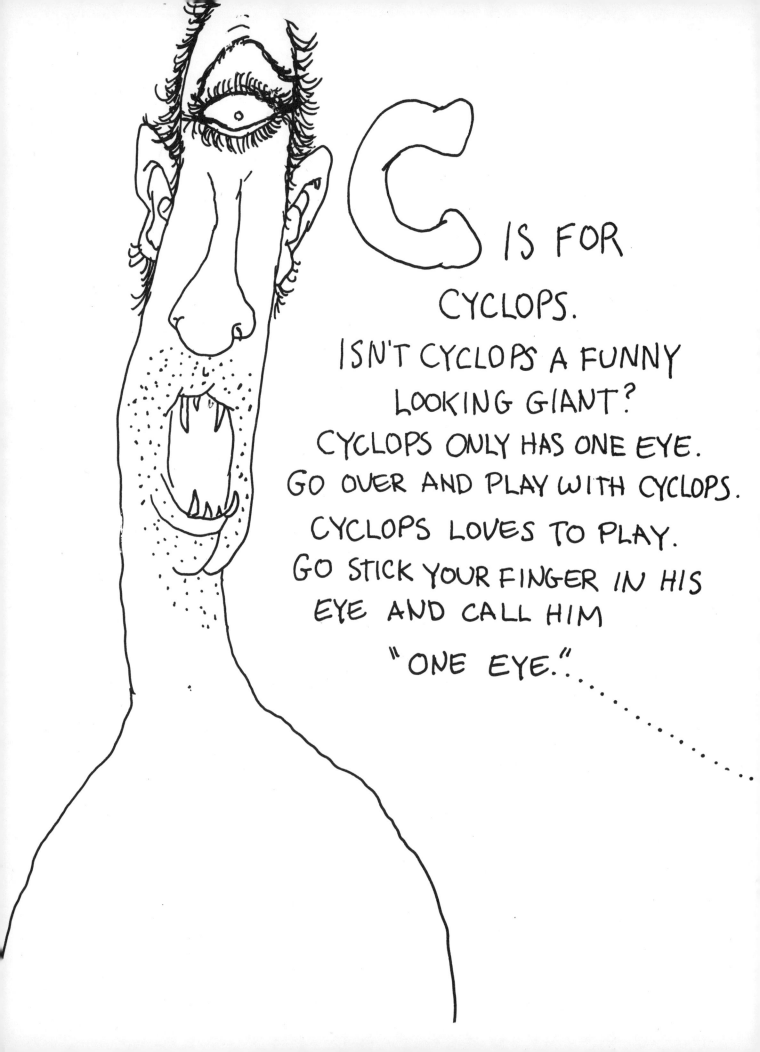

C IS FOR CYCLOPS.
ISN'T CYCLOPS A FUNNY LOOKING GIANT?
CYCLOPS ONLY HAS ONE EYE.
GO OVER AND PLAY WITH CYCLOPS.
CYCLOPS LOVES TO PLAY.
GO STICK YOUR FINGER IN HIS EYE AND CALL HIM
"ONE EYE."

I WILL WAIT HERE FOR YOU.

BECAUSE YOU HAVE BEEN GOOD,
AND BECAUSE YOUR UNCLE SHELBY LOVES YOU
TOMORROW YOU CAN STAY HOME

FROM SCHOOL

<u>NO</u> <u>SCHOOL</u> <u>TOMORROW</u>!!

WARNING !!!

IT IS NOT NICE TO BURN BOOKS
IT IS AGAINST THE LAW
IF YOUR MOMMY OR DADDY
TRIES TO BURN THIS BOOK
CALL THE <u>POLICE</u> ON THEM.

Uncle Shelby
UNCLE SHELBY.

P. S.

THE PAPER IN THIS BOOK
IS NOT REALLY PAPER...

IT IS MADE
FROM
CANDY.

THE END.